THE **CHIPMUNK WHISPERER**

VICTOR TYLER

ISBN 979-8-88644-243-4 (Paperback)
ISBN 979-8-88644-245-8 (Hardcover)
ISBN 979-8-88644-244-1 (Digital)

Covenant Books
11661 Hwy 707
Murrells Inlet, SC 29576
www.covenantbooks.com

To Patty,
my life mate of thirty-five years.
She took the chipmunk photographs.

CONTENTS

CHIPMUNK ROSTER
ALPHABETICAL ORDER

INTRODUCTION

This book is written for all the chipmunks in the USA, to inform people about this little critter in our backyards everywhere and how to have fun with them.

Chipmunks are smart, cunning, cute, adorable, playful, industrious, and trainable.

I have used the internet for some of the information in this book. I will tell you, the reader, when information comes from the internet. There is almost no information that deals with the social life in the society of chipmunks. This book will help fill that gap.

Both male and female humans can train chipmunks. This book is written to give a trainer the tools to get started. I gave all my trained chipmunks names; this made it much easier to study them. The chipmunks' names in this book are in quotations to lesson confusion in reading. I use the word-eat-in my descriptions. They do not eat the seeds I give them. They store the seeds in their cheek pouches, run home, and dump the seeds in their pantry, then come back for more.

A plus with chipmunks is, you can go on vacation and leave them alone. They are wild animals and can take care of themselves. A second plus is that when you get back home, go outside, and make your chipmunk call, you will be mobbed with enthusiasm.

I have a one-on-one experience with the chipmunk society and all the information in this book has been personally experienced.

PURPOSE OF LIFE

A chipmunk's sole purpose in life is to have babies. Nature needed food for some of her other animals and selected the very cute chipmunk.

Just like the rabbit, the chipmunk kills nothing and eats only vegetation, seeds, and berries. Chipmunks are hunted by foxes, hawks, and cats (feral cats). There is a chapter on feral cats.

Chipmunks do their best to comply with nature. In my area, the Midwest, they have babies twice a year, spring and fall. They almost always have twins. I have seen triplets only one time in twelve years.

RAISING BABIES

The internet says that the mama chipmunk will give birth to blind and hairless pups. The mother has to nurse them, keep them warm and safe.

In my chipmunk society, the mama chipmunk will come to me for food right up to delivery time. She will stop coming for ten to fifteen days. This is her nursing time.

Mama chipmunk has been very busy in her thirty-day pregnancy. She has to restock her pantry because she can't leave the pups. She has to keep her hairless pups warm and nurse them. In addition, she has to refresh the nursery with new leaves, straw, and grass.

In the last two weeks of pregnancy, she has notable weight gain. I can feel her girth growing. She is clumsy in her jumps, quick to fight, and demands her food.

EXAMPLE: When she comes for her food, she will jump from the ground up to the seat of the bench. This is an easy jump for a chipmunk. When pregnant, she does not take into account that she is extra heavy. She will miss the jump and drop to the ground.

When I see this happen, I reach down and give her a hand up to my lap for food.

After ten to fifteen days, the pups' eyes are open, and they should have a full body of hair. I have not witnessed this, but I know for a fact that a chipmunk can grow hair in one to two weeks.

OBSERVATION: When a chipmunk contracts mange, it loses all its hair in the infected area. After I treat the area, you can see the hair come back in one week; and in two weeks, you would never know the hair was missing.

Now back to Mama. She can now leave for short periods to replenish her pantry, eat, and get her fur brushed by me. In six more weeks, her pups will be the dreaded teenagers, but oh so cute!

PHYSICAL DESCRIPTION

The internet says that a chipmunk is two to five ounces and about eight to ten inches long from its head to the end of its tail. They have five toes on their front feet and four toes on the rear. Another site says the chipmunk has four toes on the front and five toes on the rear.

Okay, enough of the internet. No adult chipmunk weights two ounces. A baby, yes. When Mom turns a youngster out, it is about four ounces or more and six to seven inches long from the head to the end of its tail. As an adult one season old, it is about five to six ounces and eight to ten inches long from the head to tip of the tail. All eastern chipmunks have four toes on their front feet and five toes on the hind feet. As an adult, about 50 percent of their body weight is in the back, one-third of its body length. They stand about two inches high on all four feet. From a standing start, they can jump about twelve times their height. Their hind legs are very powerful.

Nature has given the chipmunk cheek pouches. The chipmunk uses this pouch to carry food back to its burrow. Each pouch can be opened and closed like a mouth. The pouch is dry, no saliva. Sometimes dry is a problem.

OBSERVATION: When a chipmunk eats too fast, she will choke, cough once or twice, rearrange stuff in her cheeks, and continue eating. The chipmunks also use their pouches to carry dirt when they are digging new tunnels or chambers.

The chipmunks in my area, the Midwest, have a distinctive fur pattern. They have one black stripe down their back bone, and one white stripe on each side, flanked by black stripes. This makes seven strips total.

A chipmunk's fur is as soft as mink. Nothing sticks to their fur. I tried to mark a chipmunk for identification. Marking pens would not work. I tried painting the top of a chipmunk's head with red paint. In three days, the mark was so faint I could barely make it out. Day 4, it was gone.

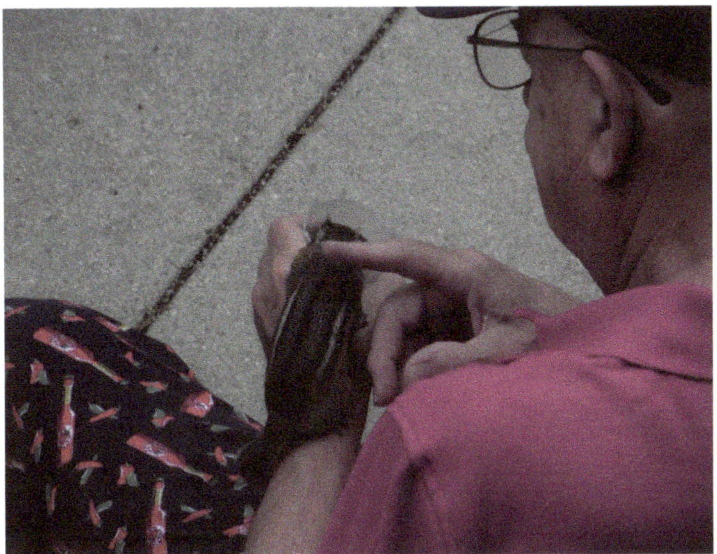

Charlene's stripes

Chipmunks do not take baths like birds. They wash themselves by licking their front feet, using them like a wash cloth and cleaning their face and head. They lick their bodies clean. They use their wet front feet like a comb, pulling their tails through them.

The chipmunks do not like rain or sprinklers. I have seen chipmunks time a sprinkler so as to dash through when the sprinkler is on the other side of the yard. They will tolerate light rain but will not come out of their burrow in stormy weather. Another thing they do not like is high wind. They will stay in their burrow if the wind is gusting or howling.

OBSERVATION: Chipmunks can see color.

One morning I went to feed the chipmunks. I made my usual call, and they came running but stopped under the bushes, flowers, and behind trees. They would not come to me. I was very puzzled. Most of the chipmunks went home. I thought and thought, everything was the same except my attire. I wore a reddish-brown polo shirt and reddish-brown pants. Fox color? Did my chipmunks think I looked like a fox? I went into the house, changed clothes, came back out, made my call, and the chipmunks came back. I was shocked. I never wore that red again to feed the chipmunks.

You can tell the age of a chipmunk with a simple test. It has to be a trained chipmunk. Have your chipmunk sit in the palm of your hand while it is eating. Wrap your fingers around the chipmunk's hind quarters and touch your fingers with your thumb. If your thumb can touch your pinky finger, it is a new chipmunk, either a spring baby or a fall baby. In either case, this chipmunk has not hibernated and is less than one year old. If you touch your ring finger, it is one year old. If you touch your middle finger, it is two years old and has finished growing. If you touch your first finger, she is pregnant. This is a simple test, and it depends on your hand size. You should check your chipmunk's size so that you can detect which female is pregnant and give them some leeway. Expect them to be feisty and give them some help in jumping. Knowing that she is pregnant, you will not be surprised or worried when she is missing. She will come back in one or two weeks. She needed to nurse her babies.

LIFE SPAN

The internet says the life span of a chipmunk is one to three years in the wild. The oldest recorded chipmunk was eight years old, but it was in captivity. The internet did not say if it was in a zoo or in someone's home. In either case, there were no predators.

In my personal experience, I have had nine live to four years old; two live to five years old; two live to six years old; and one live to eight years old so far. He is still alive and well. His name is "Duke." He has his own chapter in this book.

8 year old Duke likes grapes

SOCIAL LIFE

The social life of a chipmunk is solitude. The male and female live in their own burrows. They do not visit each other. There is NO family life. Each will fight off all visitors.

The internet says that each chipmunk claims a thirty-foot radius from its burrow entrance. I know this to be false. I have three burrows around a twenty-foot by twenty-foot patio. "Charlene" claims the west side and north side of the patio. "Newbe-3" claims the south side of the patio. "Squeak" claims the east side of the patio. When I throw birdseed on the patio, the chipmunks will come out and steal the birdseed. When two or more chipmunks come for seed, they watch each other like a hawk. Here is where you can study them and their behavior.

OBSERVATION: Let's call them chipmunks A and B. When they both come out at the same time, they start out eating the seed near their own burrow. As they follow the seed away from their burrow, they both watch each other and keep their distance from each other. Now watch closely. If A, while darting around eating seed, gets between B and her burrow, a chase will start. B will chase A all the way back to A's burrow.

OBSERVATION: Here comes a third chipmunk, C. C comes around the house to get the seed. C starts to eat the seed on the patio only to have A and B team up to chase C completely out of the yard.

Now we know chipmunks are independent, and they live in solitude. You might ask yourself how do they have kids? Good question! The DNA of a male chipmunk tells him to have sex with all the females he can. The DNA of the female tells her to have babies and raise as many as she can.

In the spring, when the female comes out of hibernation, she will go to the favorite hookup area, which is the woodpile in the backyard. She will make a high-pitched chirping sound. The male will respond, and when they are finished, she will go back to her burrow. He may stick around and make a low-pitched chirp telling other females he is available.

Neither male nor female will have anything to do with each other after mating. At eating time, rank has its privilege.

OBSERVATION: If the female is older, she will chase the male away from the food. If he is older, he will chase her away even though they just mated.

Chipmunks have a pecking order, which is by age. The oldest chipmunk, male or female, gets the food first.

EXAMPLE: A six-year-old chipmunk is eating out of a seed cup. The six-year-old fills her pouches and leaves. A two-year-old is in the area and comes over to fill her pouches. A four-year-old, in the area, comes over to fill her pouches. The four-year-old will attack the two-year-old and take over the cup. The two-year-old will hang around until the four-year-old fills up and leaves. Now the two-year-old will come back to the cup and try to fill her pouches. Well, the two-year-old is having a bad day. This time she saw the six-year-old coming back. The two-year-old takes off running. The six-year-old takes over the cup and fills her pouches then leaves. The two-year-old, for the third time, comes back to the cup, fills her pouches, and goes home. Rank has its privileges. Such is the life of a young chipmunk.

The most male chipmunks I have had in one season is three to service eighteen females. That was the year I had twenty-one trained and named chipmunks at hibernation time. The following year only eight chipmunks survived a very bad winter. The survivors were two male and six female.

The bottom line is, the male chipmunk is a cad. He impregnates as many chipmunks as he can, he lives by himself, and he has nothing to do with newborns. He only has to feed himself. He does not have to do anything except fill his pantry for the coming winter.

The female chipmunk has her own burrow. She has her pups by herself, no midwife. She nurses the pups and cleans up after them.

She switches them to pantry food and keeps them safe in her burrow. Try that with teenagers! When she thinks they are old enough, she takes them outside to the big outdoors. She trains them to find food and water. After one or two weeks, she will kick them out of her burrow. She is probably pregnant and has to get the nursery ready for her new pups.

During the one to two weeks of training, the kids are fun to watch; they have a great time outside in the new world. They keep under cover of the bushes and flowers for the most part, but you can see them chasing each other, rolling around, and just having fun. During this time, the superior will be established. The superior can be either male or female. The superior does not have to be the strongest, but has a sharper mind. A great example is "Duke." He was the runt of the litter. As he got older, his mind developed. "Duke" became the godfather to all my chipmunks.

While the new chipmunks are in training, now is a great time to start your training. The superior will come to you first and chase its sibling away. You will have to train the sibling when the superior is not present.

After the mother kicks the pups out, both siblings part ways and go forth into the new world separately. If and when the mother dies, the stronger sibling will take over her burrow.

OBSERVATION: "Charlene" had twin males in her last litter. Three weeks after "Charlene" was killed, two male chipmunks showed up at the patio. The superior took over "Charlene's" burrow—the lesser established a burrow on the east side of the patio.

The stronger I named "King." He has a chapter in this book. "King" lasted three years before a hawk got him. In one week, after "King's" death, the lesser took over "King's" burrow. His name is "Duke." "Duke" also has a chapter in this book.

So here we have "Charlene" who had two male pups. They were "King" and "Duke." "King" took over his mother's burrow. "Duke," living nearby, abandoned his burrow to take over "King's" burrow, which, if you followed this, was also the burrow of "Duke's" mother.

There is a wrinkle to all this hierarchy stuff that I have not talked about. The chipmunk society has a godfather, godmother, and a matriarch. "Charlene" came to me first because she was the godmother. I did not know this at the time I trained her. She kept the other chipmunks away. I belonged to her. When she died, her son became the godfather. This was "King." When "King" died, his brother became the new godfather.

The matriarch is not of royal blood. She is the oldest female chipmunk. When there is no godmother, she fills in. "Princess" was the matriarch. All the chipmunks in the society give way to her except the godfather. She will back down to him. The godfather backs down to nobody.

That is the way it works in the chipmunk world.

HIBERNATION

Chipmunks have a modified hibernation system. They cannot store enough fat in their body to survive the whole winter like a bear can.

The internet says that a chipmunk can lower its heart rate, breathing, and temperature. I have no way to verify this. The internet also says that a chipmunk wakes up, eats, poops, and may poke its head out of its burrow to check the weather, then go back into hibernation.

What I have observed is that a chipmunk will come out in the winter. I have fed them over the years in December, January, and February.

In the spring, when I remove the tarps covering outdoor stuff, I have found sunflower seed husks underneath. My conclusion is that yes, they do come out to check the weather. When it is tolerable, they have a picnic and leave the trash outside.

The chipmunk hibernation time in the Midwest is October to March.

Southside closed her entrance for the winter

HABITAT

Chipmunks are amazing diggers. The internet says that the chipmunk burrow can be up to thirty feet long and four feet underground with many chambers off of the main tunnel. Each chamber can be for things like a pantry, bathroom, sleeping, nursery, and rear escape hatch.

I can tell you from experience that they do have an escape hatch and a pantry. My first chipmunk, "Charlene," had her burrow in the flower bed between the house and the concrete patio. One summer day, I was putting in some stepping stones. In digging up the soil to set the stones, I dug into "Charlene's" pantry and found a lot of seeds. What was really funny was to see "Charlene" poking her head out of the destruction and giving me her evil eye. I set the stone over her pantry, and we were friends again.

Her burrow was thirty-five feet long from her escape hatch to her pantry. I have no idea what she dug under the patio.

"Charlene" moved her entrance every year, sometimes twice. When she went into hibernation, she would seal her entrance with dirt.

Duke remodeled his burrow

YARD LAYOUT

I will describe my yard layout to help make sense of some of my descriptions in this book. Of course, your yard layout will be different than mine, but it should contain the same type of areas: a hanging bird feeder, where the birds and chipmunks can eat the seed that the birds have kicked out of the feeder; an area to throw loose birdseed, like a patio or sidewalk; a bowl of water, I use a ten-inch flower pot holder and, or a bird bath; and a safe place for their rendezvous, like a woodpile, rock garden, or a fenced yard with lots of bushes in a corner.

Your feeding area should have some kind of cover behind you, like bushes, planters, wood pile, even a pile of junk, something a chipmunk can hide in and of course, a chair or a bench for you to sit on.

My backyard faces east. There is a fence between my backyard and my east neighbor's yard. This fence runs north and south and is seventy-five feet long. In front of the fence, I have bushes four feet tall. In front of the bushes are flowers. In front of the flowers is a landscape block wall eight inches tall and fifty feet long. I call this the highway. The highway starts at the north end of the property line and goes south fifty feet to the waterfall area.

From the north end of the highway, turn west along the property line. The woodpile runs west for twenty feet, then there is a sixteen-foot-long raised flower bed, twenty-four inches high. Continuing down the property line is a concrete paver pad that is six feet wide and fifty-two feet long next to the house. I have my riding mower and attachments, as well as garbage cans and storage bins on this pad next to the house. The chipmunks love this route between the stuff and the house.

I have a hanging bird feeder twelve feet from the north raised flower bed. It hangs over the edge of the pad.

The twenty-foot side of the park area is bordered on the east side by the highway. The north side has the woodpile and the raised planter. The west side has a very large maple tree with a two-seater swing hanging from a limb twenty-five feet up. The swing is on the south side of the tree facing east. There are two park benches backed up to the woodpile facing south with a storage bin in between.

The patio area is about twenty feet by twenty feet bordered by the house on the west side, the house on the north side, and a raised flower bed on the east and south side. There are ground level flower beds on the west and north sides between the house and patio. An air conditioner is off the north west corner of the patio. A fountain is to the south of the air conditioner. The glider is to the south of the fountain facing east. A step to the French doors of the house is located on the north side of the patio, at the east end. The second hanging bird feeder is on the south raised flower bed.

The waterfall is on the south east corner of the yard in a twenty-five-foot by twenty-five-foot area.

FEEDING AREA

I started out sitting on the step from the house to the patio. I would throw birdseed on the patio and discover that I had a chipmunk eating the seed. I threw a seed to her, and she ran away. When she came back, I tried to move closer to her, but she ran again. This is when I started leaving a trail of seed. This worked. Soon I had two chipmunks eating out of my hand.

I was still working at this time so I did not have a lot of time to spend on chipmunks. On the weekends, I spent a lot of time in the park. I noticed a chipmunk running up and down the highway, which was not called the highway at that time. I ended up training this chipmunk and two others to eat from the swing. If I had more than three chipmunks at the swing, they did more fighting than eating. Later I understood the pecking order.

I added the patio as a second feeding area. This worked for a while, but as I trained more chipmunks, the same thing happened— the pecking order took over. I came to realize that the older chipmunks wanted their own feeding station. I wised up. I moved my feeding area to the park area. I built a three-station feeder. It has three bowls with dividers that are four inches high. I put this on my right side within reach of my right hand so I could pet the chipmunks. On my left is the storage bin lid. I built a ramp between my legs to the ground. I use two cups to feed a chipmunk on each of my legs at the same time.

I can feed six chipmunks at once. Each chipmunk has a dedicated feeding station. I added a seventh station later. I trained a chipmunk to eat out of my shirt pocket.

New feeding area in park with cameras

The ramp chipmunks have their own positions where they like to eat. An example is "Bouncer." She liked the cup in the air. I tried to set her down on my leg, and she would leave. She had a mind of her own. I tried raising the cup. She was okay with that, but she seemed uneasy. I raised the cup up to my head. She was good with that but turned herself around to face me. That was her choice. I would bring her to about ten inches from my face and talk to her. She would stop eating and look at me as if she was trying to understand what I was saying. She would bounce her head up and down staring at me.

Your feeding area needs to be in a space big enough to expand. Please remember a trained chipmunk looks at you for trust. Give her a dedicated feeding station with black sunflower seed and she will follow you for life.

TRAINING

Training a chipmunk is not easy, but once you get the hang of it, it's not hard. Chipmunks learn from watching other chipmunks. Once you have a few trained, the others will be easier to train.

The key to training is TRUST. I will repeat this. It is extremely important. TRUST is the key to training a chipmunk.

I had help in learning how to train chipmunks; her name was "Charlene." Yes, she was a chipmunk. Please read her chapter in this book. She was my star among chipmunks.

Let's get started with training; remember TRUST. You will not make any sudden movements, sneeze, cough, yell, or lose eye contact. You will start with the proper equipment, which includes a cup (I use a laundry detergent measuring cup), black sunflower seeds, their top most favorite, and a low seat or the wall of a raised flower bed. You need to be sitting low to start. You can graduate to a chair later. Now the final ingredient, chipmunks. I am assuming that you have fed birds, either by a bird feeder or loose birdseed you have thrown out on a patio or sidewalk. In doing so, you probably have seen chipmunks eating your seed. Now you need patience.

Now that you have all the ingredients, you start by adding black sunflower seed to the birdseed in a line to where you are sitting, at least twelve feet away. Be still, this will lead the chipmunk to you. The chipmunk may dart away to unload its cheeks, but it will be back. If your line of seed is half-gone, add more seed to the line to keep her interested. Eventually she will be two or three feet away from you. You should have a little pile of seed at the end of your seed line. If she eats the pile and runs off, put less seed down. Your hand should have the seed cup an inch from the pile on the ground, tilted toward the pile. When she comes back, she will eat the pile and sniff around the cup and your very still hand. If she runs off, repeat it, but put even less food in the pile. Do not forget to talk to her in a very soft voice. Say anything. she will not understand any words but just the tone of your voice. If she leaves without eating out of the cup, do not worry; she will be back. While she is gone, put more seed down in front of the cup like before. Keep putting less seed down in front of the cup to force her into the cup. Once she starts using the cup, you may, very slowly, use your first finger to touch her on her back. She may jump away, but you must stay in your position. She will come back. Repeat this until you are petting her with your finger.

Once you have gotten this far, the next stage is getting her to eat from your hand. This step, again, will take some time. I know you are tired by now, but shake it off. While she is gone, refill the cup and change your position. You need to hold the cup on the ground like before. Here is the change. Using your second hand, put it palm up under your first hand holding the cup. When she comes back, she may sniff around, but she will go back to the cup and eat. Do not forget to pet and talk to her. Do not rush the next step. While you are feeding her, very slowly, pull your hand with the cup over your second hand while petting her. This will take many tries, but the object is to get her to step up on the fingers of your second hand while she is eating. When you get your second hand far enough for her hind legs to be in the palm of your hand, start closing your second hand around her hind end. After she comes back a few times and she is comfortable, raise both your hands about three or four inches off the ground. Repeat this a few times. When she is comfortable with this, she should place her hind end in your lower hand with no problems.

While she is this trusting, continue talking to her and maintaining eye contact. Raise her about one foot off the ground. When she is full, she will jump down. After a few trips like this, it is time to take the final step.

When she comes back, you will have both hands down. She will place her hind end in the palm of your hand, you will close your hand around her, pick her up slowly, and place your hands on your legs all the while talking to her and keeping your eyes on her. I call this movement the elevator.

Congratulations, you have now gotten your first semitrained chipmunk. At this point, I give my chipmunks a name.

You can now switch to a chair. When you call her, you will still have to lean over to pick her up, but you don't have to be slow about the pickup.

Leaning over, tapping on the cup, picking her up, talking to her, looking her in the eye—all must be performed in a smooth manner. Remember, TRUST. You must maintain her trust.

All this essential training can take three or four days. Yes, it is slow but rewarding. The next step is to get her to come up to your lap by herself. You should start her sound and sight signals. When she is in your area and you can see her, start tapping on the cup with your fingernail and saying "Come here" over and over in a soft voice. Once she is in your hand, stop both tapping and ask her, "Come here." Talk to her in your low voice as she settles her hind end into your palm and maintain eye contact with her. Close your hand around her and then pick her up to your lap and pet her from head down to her hind end. WARNING: LEAVE HER TAIL ALONE! Most chipmunks think they are being attacked from behind when their tail is touched.

I have found out that I can brush them from head to tail with my special chipmunk brush. However, I have to start at the head down to the hind end first to get her use to the brush.

The brush is an old toothbrush with the handle cut off, small enough to conceal in the palm of your hand. The sight of the brush will frighten her, so keep it concealed in your palm. Run your finger down her back a few times before you use the brush. Now use the brush by pushing in out of your palm between your first finger and thumb. Brush her from head to hind end a few times to get her used to the brush, which she cannot see. Now you should be good to go from the head all the way down to her tail.

A few days, and she will be expecting to be brushed and will get used to seeing the brush as you pull it away. Most of the time, I still hide the brush when I pick it up. At this time, you can make long strokes from head to tail. She trusts you not to hurt her.

I had many chipmunks that used the elevator. When I had my eye operation, the doctor said I could not lean over for four weeks. Not even to tie my shoes. No more elevator.

I came up with a ramp from the ground up to my park bench. The ramp is one by three inches, three feet long. The top of the ramp is between my legs and under a cushion that I sit on.

It is easy enough to get the chipmunks to come up the ramp by using the tapping trick with the cup. I found that I can train more than two chipmunks at a time. I assign them their position to eat. When both cups are occupied, the others will wait for a cup to be vacant.

I went crazy one day with too many trained chipmunks and not enough hands. I built a three-station feeding platform that sits on the right side of my bench. Now I can pet all three with my right hand. I have a storage bin on my left, and the top became one station by itself. I still had my ramp and two cups. I also trained a chipmunk to eat out of my shirt pocket. Now I was in hog heaven. I could feed seven chipmunks at a time. I trained each chipmunk to eat at its own feeding station.

The training did not take that long. It did necessitate the training of the word NO. This has proven to work very well. When a chipmunk is in the wrong station, I will say NO and give her a two-finger push. That chipmunk will leave and go to her own station.

This has proven to work with chipmunks chasing each other. I can holler NO and both chipmunks will stop in their tracks and look at me. I will point my finger at the offender and say NO again. The chipmunk being chased will continue on her way, the chaser will turn around and go on her way.

Chipmunks do not like each other and will fight for the food. However, they seem not to fight when they have assigned feeding stations.

OBSERVATION: I can feed seven chipmunks within a four-foot by two-foot area, and they will not fight. I find this remarkable.

I am amazed at what a chipmunk can learn. I have trained them with hand signals, words, and sounds. They are wild animals that deserve respect and admiration for what they can achieve.

22

FOOD

A chipmunk lives only because it stores food in its pantry, which is a chamber in its burrow. To accomplish this, they fill their pouches in their cheeks, run back to their burrow, and empty their cheeks in the pantry. They store seeds of all kinds. Soft foods, like grapes, bell peppers, etc., they eat. If you feed them a grape, they will run off with it and eat it under a bush or flower, somewhere safe. They may not eat it all, in which case, they will hide the remains and come back to finish.

I have fed chipmunks, grapes, watermelon, cantaloupe, cake, chips, shelled peanuts, and raisins. Chipmunks raid the southeast neighbor's garden and eat bell peppers. I find pieces of red and green bell peppers in the flower beds.

Their most favorite seed of all time is the black oil sunflower seed. You will have to read the chapter on "Charlene" for more details.

OBSERVATION: When a chipmunk comes to me for seed, they wash themselves, but when they eat off the ground, like under a bird feeder, they never wash. Question, do chipmunks have etiquette?

OBSERVATION: I feed the chipmunks twice a day—once in the morning and once again around four or five in the evening. I will call the chipmunks with my clicking sound, and they come running. An older chipmunk (older is three or more years), will jump up to the food cup, pause, then gently nibble my finger before eating. Is this a good morning handshake? The nibble is only in the morning, never hard and only for the first trip. That chipmunk will make many more trips for food that day with no more nibbling. This has happened to many of the old-timers. Is this a form of appreciation?

You can pat yourself on the back when a chipmunk actually cracks open a black seed while in your hand and eats the contents. This shows that she has total trust in you. Congratulations!

THE YARD OF DEATH

I have chipmunks coming from all over the neighborhood. Our house faces west. We have neighbors on the lot south, southeast, east, northeast, north, and far north. That's seven lots with houses, counting ours.

One house I call the house of death. This house is on the southeast lot. There is a large vegetable garden in the yard. Chipmunks and squirrels love this patch of ground. The chipmunks go after the bell peppers, the best in the garden. There is no way for me to stop the chipmunks from partaking in this feast. My neighbor in this house is upset to say the least. He has a solution: set traps. He uses mouse traps baited with peanut butter. A very effective solution. I can't blame him for this practice; the chipmunks are the invaders. To this day I will not feed my chipmunks peanut butter. I do not want them to crave the taste.

MEDICAL

Chipmunks have no communicable diseases. They can pick up ticks, which do carry diseases.

Some internet sites list all kinds of diseases that a chipmunk can carry, scaring you into believing that a chipmunk bite can give you a disease. Wrong!

Chipmunks can pick up ticks in the grass, bushes, and flowers. The tick can jump to the chipmunk and then to you. The tick would then have to bite you to give you trouble. Ticks come from other animals, usually deer.

In order for you to have ticks in your yard, a deer, fox, raccoon, or some other forest-dwelling animal would have to lie down in your yard or go through your bushes so that the ticks can jump off or be brushed off. The tick would have to have bitten a sick animal prior to his jumping off in your yard. Not all ticks carry a disease. The bottom line is, if you are afraid of ticks, and your area is prone to ticks, leave chipmunks alone.

The only sickness I have observed is mange. When a chipmunk contracts mange, it means death to the little critter. Without her fur, she will freeze to death in the winter.

Mange is from a mite that feeds off the hair roots of mammals, dogs, cats, horses, and chipmunks.

My first case of mange was on a chipmunk. I noticed the hair was missing on her neck, about the size of a pencil. I thought she had been bitten in a fight. I watched it closely. The skin was not broken, just missing hair. The area grew, and two more spots opened up with no hair. I called a vet and asked if he knew of a medicine I could use to stop the mange. He was no help. He said bring it in, and he would look at the chipmunk. I called the village animal control, and they said to call the county animal control. No help. I called the state animal control, national wildlife, and the regional animal control. None of these had any answers.

I went to the internet. There, solution was shots. The animal would be weighed and given a shot, so many CC of serum per pound. This was no answer, as a chipmunk weighs four to seven ounces.

All this took about three weeks. I had to wait for callbacks or some sort of response from each agency.

Now we are talking about a massive spread of mange on this poor chipmunk. Desperate, I went to PetSmart to find something I could use on my chipmunk. The clerk was understanding but could only offer a spray. I could not use a spray because the spray would get in the chipmunk's eyes, plus it would scare the crap out of the little chipmunk. I would lose all the trust that this chipmunk had in me. The clerk said that they had a roving specialist that went from store to store and happened to be in this store today. The clerk went to get her. I explained my problem to the doctor, who was very interested in what I wanted to do. She said, of course, a spray would not do. She said I would need a powder or a liquid to apply directly on the mange. I said that would not be a problem because I can hold and pet these chipmunks. The doctor said she did not have a powder that was suitable, but she had a liquid in a tube that might work. It was a flea and tick squeeze-on for cats. She said it had some of the ingredients that kills the mite that causes mange.

By now, my poor chipmunk "Highway" had three spots around her neck, a large spot on each of her sides, and another large spot on her back. Six spots total.

The first time I used the medication was at the morning feeding. I put one drop on her side. She took off like I shot her. Did I hurt her? Did it sting? Was it cold? Will she come back? I continued feeding the other chipmunks while I waited. About ten minutes later, she came back. Her hair around the hole was all matted down, and she smelled like medicine. The liquid had been absorbed by the hair and skin around the hole. I gave her another dose on her other side. She kept coming back, and I kept dosing her. When I finished, she looked like a wet rat. It took about a week to see that the hair was coming back. She had no new holes; her hair grew back in two weeks.

I had cured her, thanks to PetSmart. At this point, I will give PetSmart a huge thank you for listening to me and caring. The product is listed below.

The company name is ONLY NATURAL PET.

The product is EASY DEFENCE FLEA AND TICK SQUEEZ-ON FOR CATS.

Over the years I have treated many chipmunks. All have survived the mange.

THE YARD OF SICKNESS

Over the years, I have treated chipmunks for mange. All these cases have been chipmunks that live in the lot south. The house has been expanded to include a water reclamation system, which includes large underground tanks in the ground (front and rear), to collect water runoff. This is used by the sprinkler system for the grass. Every house should have one.

OBSERVATION: All my sick chipmunks smell like sewer. Could there be a connection? I don't know, but I wonder if the mite that causes mange lives in that system.

Oh well, I have the medication and will continue to use as needed. It works.

FERAL CATS

The internet says that a feral cat is a cat that has had very little human contact. Such as an owner turning a cat out in the morning and taking the cat back in for the evening. This type of cat can be introduced into a male feral cat harem and have wild-born kittens. Once an adult cat has turned wild, it will never turn back into a house cat. They eat whatever they can catch, such as birds, mice, rabbits, chipmunks, and even squirrels.

I have a HAVE-A-HEART trap to catch these cats. I turn the cats over to animal control in our village. The officer told me that the cats are worthless as a house pet, and they euthanize this type of cat.

One such catch was a huge cat that filled the cage. I was moving the cage out into the yard so animal control could pick it up easily. As I was moving the cage, this cat tore open the door and bit my foot right through my shoe, sole and all, then ran off. I went to the emergency room, and the doctor gave me a shot for a disease that a feral cat can have in its saliva.

Later, in one of the officer's trips, he told me to cover the trap with a cloth. This way, the animal can't see and can be moved safely. He also told me to just leave the trap alone, and he would take care of it. Good to know. We learn by our mistakes.

NAMING CHIPMUNKS

Naming a chipmunk is essential to studying them. They have likes and dislikes just like humans. You can be a better host or hostess if you take the time to know your chipmunk.

OBSERVATION: My chipmunk "Charlene" knew many hand signals. I would tap my hand on the seat next to me while I was swinging, and she would jump up next to me, stretch out across the swing slats, belly down, legs spread out, and look out over the yard while I am petting her. "Charlene's" reward was not food related but companionship.

Chipmunks give signals also.

OBSERVATION: "Duke" would jump up to his empty feeding station. I was busy with other chipmunks and did not notice "Duke" or his empty food station. "Duke" would poke me on my left arm and look at me. When we made eye contact, he would turn his head and look at the empty food station then look back at me. This is his signal to me.

Signals are there. We just have to be observant and get to know our chipmunks. Naming them makes you recognize them as an individual. They are different.

Dreaming up a name was hard for me. I started to use their physical flaws like a crooked tail, nick in one ear, rings in the tail, and other such flaws. I use their mannerisms—shy, bold, pushy, and the like. I have a list of the royal hierarchy for "Princess's" offspring. I use their burrow location, the path they use to go home, and other factors—the list is limited only by your imagination. I have used ninety-one names so far. As a general rule, when a chipmunk dies, its name is retired. By the way, this makes record keeping much easier.

CHARLENE

LIVED SIX YEARS

"Charlene" was my first chipmunk. She trained me as much as I trained her. I started just like the chapter on TRAINING teaches you—I gave up the coffee can for a cup, as I explain later. I got her to come to the can and eat birdseed while I pet her.

OBSERVATION: This method has worked well for twelve years.

I named him "Charley." HA! This is before I read a bunch of stuff about chipmunks on the internet, some true, some false, and some stupid. I did learn that "Charley" was a female chipmunk. I changed her name to "Charlene" and now refer to him as her.

At this point I hope you have read the chapter on YARD LAYOUT. I make reference to different locations with names to simplify descriptions, like park, highway, patio, raised bed, swing, glider, etc. Let's get back to "Charlene's" story.

One day, twelve years ago, I was in the swing and saw a chipmunk running down the highway to the woodpile. I decided to see if I could feed this critter. I had been feeding two chipmunks on the patio for two years. I put a can of birdseed right next to the highway so that the chipmunk would run right by the can and maybe stop to check it out. This did not work, so I put some seed on top of the highway to make her stop. This worked. She came back to the can a few times. At this point I am in the swing twenty-five feet away from the can. I moved the can three feet away from the highway. Now she would have to jump down off the highway to get to the can. She did jump down and walk all the way around the can, sniffing. Finally she jumped into the can. I let her come back twice before I moved the can another three feet away. I kept this up until the can was even with the side of the swing. I even swung while she was in the can. Once she got used to all this, I put the can on the end of the swing. When she came back, she looked for the can all around the ground. She finally saw the can on the edge of the swing. I kept the swing still at this time. She jumped up on the swing, checked things out, and jumped into the can. While she was gone to unload her cheeks, I moved the can closer to me, then closer, then closer, until the can was next to me. I put my right hand on the rim of the can. She did not like this move, but she jumped into the can anyway. I put my hand into the can so she would have to touch me to eat. You should know the drill by now. Baby steps. I was able to pet her while she ate.

I noticed that she was eating the black sunflower seeds out of the birdseed first. She seemed to be digging to get this seed. I used my hand while she was still in the can and churned up the seed in the can to bring up the black seed. She caught on quickly and would actually wait for me to do so.

All this time I was stopping the swing so she could jump up. One day she jumped on the swing while I was swinging. Her timing was great. After that I no longer stopped the swing.

It was around this time that I realized this is one of the two chipmunks that I had been feeding on the patio, off and on, for two years. At that time, I called her "Charley." This was before I got serious about training and studying chipmunks.

When I swing for pleasure, I put a cushion against the arm rest, put my back on the cushion, and stretch my legs out on the seat with my feet under the other arm rest. One day I was chilling out and swinging when I felt a thump at my feet. "Charlene" had jumped up on the swing and climbed up my shoe. She held on to my toes with her front feet, straddled my shoelaces with her hind legs, and laid her body down. She swung with me for at least ten minutes, not a care in the world. She did this often. I had no feeding schedule set up. I would swing after I finished yard work. She would find me and invite herself. This was friendship with no expectations.

Charlene and me swinging

One sunny day I was feeding her on the swing. We were swing-ing, I was petting her while she was eating in the can. She made a loud squeal, jumped straight up out of the can over my head past the swing chains to the ground, and took off running. I had no idea what just happened and was very glad she did not break any bones. She had to have dropped five feet to the ground. She came back the next day, and everything was fine for a while. It happened again a few days later. I studied the can and seed. I could not see anything wrong. I had my head in the can when I pushed off to set the swing in motion. That is when a blinding flash hit me in the face. I figured it out. The sun was bright that day. The swing was in the shade except some light got through the leaves of the tree. When I swung, those patches of sun-light hit the inside of the can. This causes a flash of light like a flash bulb going off in your face. She must have thought the world blew up.

This is why I only feed chipmunks with a plastic cup. This is also about the time I started feeding the chipmunks black sunflower seeds. To prove to myself that black sunflower seed was her favorite, I filled one cup with birdseed and a second cup with black sunflower seed. I held both cups in one hand with the birdseed cup closest to the chip-munk so that she would get the birdseed cup first. When "Charlene" jumped up for her snack, she sniffed the birdseed cup, then climbed over the first cup to get to the black sunflower seed cup. I did this test many times with other chipmunks. The results were always the same—chipmunks prefer the black sunflower seed over birdseed.

"Charlene" taught me my chipmunk call. One day she was on the woodpile chirping. I went over to see her. She looked at me but still chirped. I offered her the seed cup, but she refused. I clicked using my tongue on the roof of my mouth. She gave me a look but kept on chirping. She would chirp, then I would click. This went on for quite a while. She finally quit and went away. To this day I use that click to call the chipmunks. The chipmunks learned that the click is my call to them. If they are out of their burrow and within earshot, they will come running.

By the way, I later found out that her chirp was a mating call and the woodpile was the rendezvous point. I guess she was quite annoyed at me interfering with her call.

"Charlene" got quite used to eating out of the cup to the point where she used it for amusement. In my left hand, I held the cup between my first finger and thumb with the web of my hand wrapped around the cup. She would jump to my wrist, lie down, hold on to the cup with her front feet, and chew on the cup, either for pleasure or to sharpen her teeth. I never figured out which. She destroyed three cups in her lifetime. She did not eat the pieces she chewed off, they just dropped all over me.

When she finished chewing, she would stand up and wait for me to move my right hand up next to the cup. She would move over to the palm of my right hand and sit down. She would hold the cup with both front feet and eat her fill. When she came back, she would skip the cup chewing.

The first time I was bitten was by "Charlene." I was holding the cup as usual but did not pay attention as to how far the cup had ben chewed down. It was almost half-gone. The web of my hand was very near the edge. She was chewing on the cup when I felt pain. I flinched, and she jumped down on the glider seat and looked at me. I squeezed the puncture, which stopped the bleeding. I picked up the cup, gave "Charlene" the hand signal, a tap on my wrist, that it was okay to eat. She was sitting there the whole time, watching. She came back up slowly looking at me while she positioned herself in her eating position. She kept looking at me to see if I was okay, but maybe she was worried that I was going to smack the crap out of her. I chose to think that it was concern.

Way before this incident, "Charlene" had learned a hand signal. Normally I would click for her to come to the cup. Sometimes she was too far away to hear the click or the noise level was too high and she could not hear the click. I started clicking and tapping my left wrist with the first finger of my right hand. I did this for a while. One day I saw her and just tapped my wrist, then she came running. From then on, she would come with just a tap. I trained many other chipmunks with hand signals. Chipmunks are smart.

All this time I am learning about chipmunks, I only trained "Charlene." I kept her exclusive because I thought she might resent me playing with other chipmunks. If she was on the ground in front of me, she would chase all the chipmunks that came in the area. When she was in my lap, on the swing, in my hands, she would let them be. Could this be a possessive move? Or could this be a this-is-my-area-stay-out move? I do know that with feeding stations, the chipmunks are more tolerant with each other.

"Charlene" was killed by a feral cat. Feral cats are domestic cats that are no longer wanted and turned loose. They revert back to the wild very quickly. See the chapter on feral cats. The cat killed three chipmunks at the same time, "South Side," "Red Butt," and "Charlene." I did not see this happen. This is what I think happened. "Charlene" and "South Side" would team up to chase other chipmunks off the patio. "Red Butt" was no exception. "South Side" and "Charlene" are patio chipmunks; "Red Butt" is from the north house lot. The patio chipmunks teamed up to chase the invader, "Red Butt," out of their area. All three are chasing in line as usual. The cat catches "Red Butt" first, then it hits and kills "South Side" and lunges for "Charlene," breaking her back or hip. "Charlene" gets away.

I came home from work and went out to feed the chipmunks. I called and nobody came. I was sitting on the patio glider and saw a slow movement on the left side of the glider. It was "Charlene."

Her burrow was eight inches from the back of the glider. She pulled herself over to the spot where she normally jumps up on the glider. She gave me a long look, I talked to her and reached down under the arm of the glider but could not reach her. I got up and went around the glider and down to her level. I was going to pet her, but I stopped when I saw how badly she was hurt. She gave me a last look, like apologizing for not jumping up. She turned and crawled back to her burrow, which was eight inches away. I never saw her again. I will always remember the last look she gave me, so haunting.

The next day I found "Red Butt's" skin with fur, no flesh or bone, just skin. I never found "South Side." The cat probably took her home to her babies.

I have many GREAT memories with "Charlene," things she taught me. The best was companionship. The times she would come on the glider and chew on her cup. I still have two of those cups. The times she would jump up on the swing and sit on my shoe just to enjoy swinging. The times she would straddle my wrist with her front feet on the cup, body flat out on my hand, on the glider or swing, ignoring the food and enjoying the back-and-forth movement.

The time I came back from vacation and sat on the glider, she was on the highway about a hundred feet away when she heard my clicking. She stopped dead in her tracks, stood on her hind legs, twisting her head around to figure out where the sound was coming from. I clicked again. She zeroed in on the sound and saw me. She came running across the yard, screaming like I have never heard before. She screamed all the way to the patio, made two running jumps across the patio, one more jump to the glider seat, then one more to my wrist. I held her, petted her, and talked to her. I could feel her purring. This was my first experience with purring from a chipmunk. Yes, a chipmunk can purr, but you can't hear the purr, you can only feel her purring. I have felt this many times with other chipmunks.

"Charlene" is etched in my memory forever.

RED BUTT

LIVED ONE YEAR

The chipmunks in this chapter are "Red Butt," female, lived one year; "Red Butt Jr.," female, lived three years; "The Kid," male, lived two years; and "South Side," female, lived one year.

I named her "Red Butt" because her reddish-brown hind end was redder than any other chipmunk. With other chipmunks around, anybody could pick out "Red Butt."

I trained "Red Butt" to eat out of a cup when "Charlene" was not around. "Red Butt" was bold and courageous. She knew the patio birdseed was off limits, but she did not care. She would announce her comings before she came around the corner of the house to the patio.

Oooh! That feels nice.

"Red Butt" would jump up on the raised flower bed and check things out. She had three options:

1. Was "Charlene" out? If so "Red Butt" would sit and wait.
2. Was "Charlene" up on the glider with me? Then "Red Butt" would jump down and eat birdseed.
3. If "Charlene" was not around, "Red Butt" would come to me on the glider and eat black seed.

Now the wild card was "South Side," a much more laid-back chipmunk. When "Red Butt" would make her announcement that she was coming, "South Side" would go home if "Charlene" was not around. "Red Butt" would eat birdseed or come to me for black seed. If "Charlene" was eating out of her cup with me on the glider, "South Side" would stay out and let "Red Butt" eat the birdseed. "South Side" kept a close eye on her, but if "Red Butt" got too close or got between "South Side" and her burrow, "South Side" would attack "Red Butt," and "Charlene" would jump down and help give chase. This was a daily ritual, whether I was there or not.

I am very sure this is how the cat got all three chipmunks. They ran right into the cat's mouth and claws. I found "Red Butt's" skin a day later, all the flesh and bones were gone and only the skin was left.

"Red Butt" was with me for only one season, but she did have a kid. I named her "Red Butt Jr." in her mother's honor. The kid had a hind end as red as her mother's. "Red Butt's" kid took over her burrow and used the same path to go home; however, "Red Butt Jr." had no odd quirks from the original "Red Butt."

This "Red Butt Jr." liked the swing. She would jump up on the swing like "Charlene" but only to eat. When she was pregnant, she would miss her jumps and slam her body into the swing. This led me to add a ramp to one side of the swing, which came down from the seat to about four inches off the ground. She soon learned to jump to the ramp, then climb up to me. After "Red Butt Jr." had her ten-day maternity leave, she came back for seed for her kids. I noticed that she was making a lot of trips. The next day, I timed her from my cup to her burrow and back. It was three minutes, which included pouch-filling time. That day she made thirty-two trips before she quit. "Red Butt Jr." was with me for three years. She was a great mother. I trained her first baby, named him "The Kid," red hind end and all. I could not name him "Red Butt" because his mother was still alive. "The Kid" lasted for two years.

KING

LIVED THREE YEARS

"Charlene's" last babies were twin males. In the chipmunk world, when the mother dies, the strongest sibling takes over the burrow. In this case, "King" took over "Charlene's" burrow. "King's" brother "Duke" made a new burrow on the east side of the patio. "King" tolerated "Duke" but only so-so. I gave "King" his name after King Henry VIII. "King" dominated everything and everyone in the chipmunk society. "Charlene" was the godmother while she was alive. The pecking order in the chipmunk society gave "King" the godfather status even though he was less than one year old.

There is a birdbath in the patio area, and "Charlene" would sit on the foot of the pedestal like a throne. "King" did the same thing. He overlooked the patio, like he dared anyone to eat his birdseed on the patio. One day, I saw "King" chase a squirrel off the patio. That took guts. He did allow the birds to eat the birdseed.

I would sit on the glider on the patio to feed the birds. I trained "King" to jump up on the left side of the glider. I would feed him out of a cup. "King," like his mother, learned the hand signal to come and swing. He would spread out on the slats, and I would pet him—no food, just companionship.

"Duke" has his own chapter in this book, but I have to bring him into this story because "Duke" is the sole reason I had to train "King" to the word NO. "Duke" was damaged at birth with a hip problem. He did not move fast. He was also shy, and he respected his brother's control.

I finely trained "Duke" to eat out of a cup on the ground between my shoes when I was on the glider. "Duke" would not come up on the glider. There were times I was feeding both, "King" on the glider and "Duke" on the ground between my shoes.

"Duke" would not come to his cup if "King" was around. "Duke" was smart. He figured out that "King" could not see him while I was feeding "King." "Duke" would sneak in from the right side of the glider then under the glider to my shoes and to the cup of seed.

"King" finally caught "Duke" eating on the ground but did not chase. When "King" came back for seed, he did not jump up on the glider but went to my shoes, to "Duke's" cup and ate "Duke's" seed. This happened a couple of times, then I took action. I leaned over and pushed "King" away from the cup with the back of my hand. He kept coming back. I kept pushing him away but added the word NO. At one point, after I pushed him away, he turned around and bared his teeth at me. I quickly used two fingers and clipped "King" under his jaw and said NO loudly. Then I pointed my finger at him and said NO again. He walked away and jumped up to his cup and ate. I petted him as usual. Meanwhile, "Duke" came over and ate out of his cup on the ground.

When "King" came back for a refill, he did the same thing. He went for "Duke's" cup. I leaned over, said NO, and pushed him away. He turned around to come back, and I pointed at him and said NO loudly. He then came to his cup by my side. This went on a couple more times. It got to a point where I would say NO and point at him. He would stop.

This was a milestone in training, and "Duke" was the sole reason that I achieved this level of training.

Later, I got "King" eating on my left side and "Duke" eating on my right side, on the glider, at the same time.

Gripping King

"King" only lasted three years. My guess is that a hawk got him. Soon after, about two weeks, "Duke" took over "King's" burrow and duties as godfather.

DUKE

EIGHT YEARS OLD AND STILL ALIVE

"Duke" is the lesser of the twin males of "Charlene." "Duke" set up his burrow on the east side of the patio. I started training both "Duke" and "King" about the same time.

"Duke" was slow and reserved. He did not like eating the birdseed on the patio because his brother "King" was a bully. I sat on a chair next to the raised flower bed on the east side of the patio. This put me very close to "Duke's" burrow entrance. I put seed on top of the wall of the raised bed just for "Duke." I did the usual training and got "Duke" to eat out of a cup in my hand. He got very comfortable with me. I was able to sit on the glider and get him to come to me if I leaned over to feed him. When he filled up, he would stroll home. This is when I noticed his problem. "Duke's" walk was a stroll. His little hind end swung back and forth, just like the Western movie star John Wayne. John Wayne's nickname was "the Duke." This is how "Duke" got his name. As for running, "Duke" learned how to hop-run. That's to say, he did not run four-legged style. He ran like a cheetah. He launched himself with both rear legs, his front legs are reaching forward. When his front legs hit the ground, they are pulling his body forward while the rear legs are in the air moving forward. When the rear legs hit the ground, the front legs are in the air reaching forward, ready for the rear leg launch. This gives him a hopping run, very distinctive and very fast.

"Duke" is a very gentle soul. He is the only chipmunk that I have trained that cared about female chipmunks.

One day I was feeding "Duke" from a chair on the patio. He filled his cheeks as usual, turned to go home, but did not. He jumped down from the raised bed and went over to the waterfall area.

I need you to understand, male chipmunks service female chipmunks, period. That is their sole purpose. No attachments. "King" services the females north and east at the woodpile. "Duke" services the female chipmunks east and south at the waterfall. This is how they set themself up in their duties.

Now back to "Duke." He went to the waterfall area with full cheeks. A short time later he returned with empty cheeks. I fed him again, and he did the same thing, turned and went back to the waterfall area with full cheeks and returned with empty cheeks. "Duke" did this five times before he filled up his cheeks for himself and went home. How this figures in with the chipmunk society, I cannot understand. Not yet. "Duke" did this for only one spring season.

When "King" died, "Duke" took over "King's" burrow, which, as you know by now, belonged to his mother, "Charlene." "King" had moved the burrow entrance many times just like his mother did. "Duke" was no exception. Over the years, "Duke" moved the entrance many more times.

"Duke" let his feelings show again. He took in an orphaned chipmunk.

A female chipmunk had a burrow in front of our house. She would come to the patio in the evening for birdseed. She came every evening and ran every time I tried to step on the patio. I did not know she was feeding babies. She was untrained, and I did not take the time to train her. It would have taken a lot of time. I made sure there was birdseed on the patio every evening. She made regular trips. As time passed, I did not pay her much attention. Then one day I saw "Duke" running back and forth to the front. Once again, I was shocked by "Duke's" behavior. A male chipmunk just does not care for a female. It was a week later that I saw a baby chipmunk poke her nose out of "Duke's" burrow. As it turned out, the unnamed female chipmunk was killed. I never saw her again. She left a baby in her burrow. "Duke," the father, took over feeding the little one. When the little one was old enough, "Duke" moved her to his burrow and finished raising the kid. I saw the baby come out of "Duke's" burrow many times only to be ushered back in by "Duke." A few weeks later, "Duke" let her out to explore but kept a close eye on her. One day, the baby was gone, I never saw her again.

OBSERVATION: "Duke" has a sense of family duty that I have not observed in any male chipmunk in my twelve years of observing.

"Duke" has been fed in many places. He was taking the changes well except for one. He would NOT come up on the swing. I could reach down and feed him out of a cup, but as soon as I try to pick him up, he would jump out of my hand. I would give him the hand signal to come sit next to me, like I do for the glider on the patio, which he loves, but he would not have anything to do with the swing. When I am feeding other chipmunks on the swing, "Duke" would come over and pick up dropped seed. I made a game out of this. I would drop seed on top of his head while swinging. He would scramble around picking up every seed.

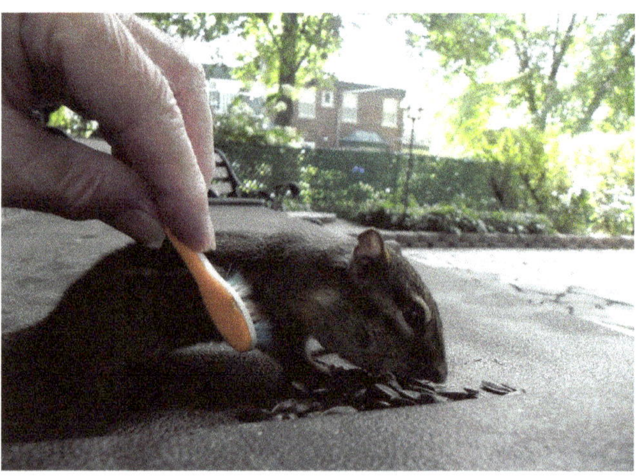

Brushing Duke at his feeding station

When I built the large feeding stations in the park, "Duke" and I picked out the top of the storage bin. It is next to me. I can pet and brush him. He can defend his station with ease. He can come and go as he pleases, and I put seeds out for him on request. All the other chipmunks know that it is "Duke's" feeding station. If another chipmunk tries to eat as "Duke's" I shoo them away. When "Duke" is eating, he can feel the vibrations of another chipmunk walking on top of the storage bin. "Duke" will turn around quickly and chase the invader off the bin top but no farther. When he comes back to his station, sometimes the seed is spread over the bin top by his tail. I will grab his body and push him around the bin top to pick up the scattered seed, like a vacuum cleaner.

"Duke" and I have an understanding. I put seed down when he is there. If I do not pay attention and let the seed run out, "Duke" will poke my left arm. When I turn around, he will make eye contact, turn his head, and point at his station; he will pause then look at me again. Of course, I pour more seed. At this point, who has trained who?

One morning, "Duke" came late as usual; he is not an early riser. He had not come for a couple of days. This was not unusual for a four-year-old male. This day was different. "Duke" did not pounce on the bin top as usual. He just wandered over to his food, lay down on his belly, and picked at his seed. When I petted him, I could feel each rib and back bone. He was skin and bone. I petted him and talked to him. He looked at me like his mother did just before she died. "Duke" stood up and walked away without filling his cheeks. I saw him go to his burrow.

He did not come back. I watched his burrow for weeks. The only good sign was that his entrance was not closed up and no chipmunk had taken over his burrow.

I was feeding chipmunks on the patio about five weeks later when a chipmunk poked its nose out of "Duke's" burrow. When he came out of the burrow, I could see the short tail. It was "Duke." He looked like he was drugged. He staggered around and walked sideways. I called him only to be ignored. He went back to his burrow.

Next morning, I saw no activity in "Duke's" burrow. I went to feed the other chipmunks and about thirty minutes later, "Duke" jumped down from the bin top making quite a racket. He looked at me, like "Where is my food?" I poured his seed, petted him, and talked to him while he ate. He had gained almost all his weight back. His loose skin filled out. He was almost back to normal. I was elated.

"Duke" got sick again two years later. Another chipmunk used the same entrance to "Duke's" burrow. I thought "Duke" was a goner. A couple weeks later, there were two chipmunks using "Duke's" burrow. It was "Duke" and a stranger. I ended up training the newcomer and named him "Caretaker." He seemed to take care of "Duke."

"Duke" got better in a few more weeks. After which, "Caretaker" made a new entrance to the burrow on the right side of the backdoor step. "Duke's" entrance was on the left side of the step, which both of the chipmunks used while "Duke" was sick and recuperating. When "Caretaker" made his new entrance, "Duke" closed up his entrance and moved it behind the air conditioner. It looked like they split up the tunnels. Another first for me—both males and no fighting.

"Duke" learned words. He understood "COME HERE." He also understood a stretched out NOOOO, softly said, and a sharply said NO. He also learned "DUKE, COME HERE," when said sharply. I would say this when he is chasing chipmunks around the park area. He would stop even if he was out of sight and come up to his station.

"Duke" is the godfather of my chipmunk society. He is now eight years old and doing very well.

RENEGADE

LIVED ONE YEAR

The time frame was back when I sat in a chair on the patio to feed "Duke" at his first burrow in the south-raised flower bed. "Duke" was already trained to the cup and black seed. I would leave seed on top of the raised bed for "Duke."

"Renegade" was a chipmunk from the front of the house on the south lot. She made her run through the bushes, trees, and flowers on the property line to get to the birdseed on the patio. I noticed that "Renegade" would steal "Duke's" seed on the raised bed if I left the seed unattended. Once in a while, "Duke" would catch "Renegade" stealing his seed. "Duke" would run, chasing "Renegade" out of the yard.

I trained "Renegade" to the cup when "Duke" was not around. At this time, I was using only one cup, which was a big mistake. I was feeding "Renegade" when "Duke" showed up. "Duke" attacked "Renegade" with a vengeance. "Renegade" did not run as usual. They both fought like they were going to kill each other. I reached over to break up the fight, and Renegade bit me on my finger. I hollered NO and pushed "Renegade" with two fingers. "Duke" knew the word and just stopped. "Renegade" ran home.

In hindsight, I now know that "Duke" thought "Renegade" was eating the seed out of his cup, and "Renegade" thought "Duke" was going to steal her seed.

This was the second time I was bitten by a chipmunk. The bite was not directed at me, it was an accident. A chipmunk's teeth are very sharp. A bandage was needed to stop the bleeding.

Later, "Renegade" came back, and I fed her out of my hand, not the cup. With a little more training, I could feed both chipmunks at the same time with no fighting, "Duke" out of his cup and "Renegade" out of my hand.

Tell me more

At the end of summer, I found "Renegade" dead in the yard on the path she used to come to me. She had no marks on her except her throat was cut. It looked like she was on her route to the birdseed when a landscaper next door, using a string trimmer, caught "Renegade" zigging instead of zagging and cut her throat. She ran about ten feet into my yard and dropped dead.

PRINCESS

LIVED SIX YEARS

"Princess" lived at the front of the north house. I have a six-foot property line set back. I paved this strip along the entire north side of the house (see the chapter on yard layout). The north house also has a six-foot set back but in grass. I park my riding mower on the pad near the front of the house.

"Princess" travels from the front of the north house, crosses the twelve feet between the houses and scoots next to the house down the north side, jumps up on the planter, runs its length, jumps down to the park then jumps up to my bench and to her feeding station, which is the middle bowl of three. This is where I feed her extra food like grapes, shelled peanuts, and raisins. Many times, she will refuse these soft foods and just store the black seed. When she does take the soft food, she will eat it on the spot, not run off to eat like most chipmunks.

Her feeding station is in the middle of three stations and has a divider on two sides. When she wants to be brushed, not just petted, she will stand on her hind legs and put her front feet on top of the divider, stretching herself out. I can reach the entire length of her body. I brush from her eyebrows down to her tail then each side of her body. She is calling the shots. She is telling me this is what she wants. When she has had enough, she will jump back down and finish eating. I can be brushing her for five to ten minutes. HA! Who has trained who?

Petting Princess at her feeding station

"Princess" will not attack the other chipmunks eating in the bowls north and south of her just one inch away. The dividers define the space. No chipmunk would dare to eat out of "Princess's" bowl; she was the matriarch of the chipmunk society.

"Princess" had four babies a year, two in the spring and two in the fall. None survived their first year except two, and they only lived for two years each. I trained most of her babies only to have the hawks eat them. See the chapter on "Dumb Shit" for one of the survivors. The other survivor was "Alcove."

"Alcove" wanted me to feed her. She would only use the ramp and only if a cup was available. Her position that she picked was on either hand, left or right, in the air, eye to eye. She wanted me to talk to her and stroke her back.

One year, we had a very bad winter. Twenty-one trained chipmunks went into hibernation and only eight made it back. "Princess" was one of the eight. I remember her first trip out of hibernation. I had made my call to the chipmunks, and I was looking to see who would be coming. I saw "Princess" come flying around the north house, down the pad. She did not jump up on the raised planter; she went straight to my bench, jumped up on the bench, leaped into her bowl, and looked at me. I reached over and petted her. It was like no time had passed. She remembered everything.

Around April, I could tell she was pregnant. She got big as a house, as the saying goes. One morning, she did not show up for her feeding. I figured she was having her babies and would be gone for two weeks. "Princess" never came back. The matriarch was gone at six years old and going on seven. I am quite sure the hawk got her.

I have many great memories of "Princess."

DUMB SHIT

LIVED ONE YEAR

In one of "Princess's" six years, she had two kids that did not survive the summer. This is their story.

These kids played under the north bird feeder located near the raised flower bed next to the park. I started my usual training with the black seed trail from the bird feeder to the raised flower bed. I sat on the wall of this planter. There is two feet of red brick between the planter and the concrete pad. One of the babies followed the seed, filled up, went home, emptied, and came back to the bird feeder. She did not come back to the trail where she left off. I replaced the seed trail. She ate the trail, filled up, went home, and came back to the bird feeder again. This went on until I quit.

The next day, I did the same all over again. This time, she did follow the seed trail, coming back to where she left off. She stopped at the brick and would not cross over. I moved as close to the end of the planter as I could, sat on the edge, and reached out with a handful of seed. She ate out of my hand but would not step off the pad.

The third day I started over again and got her eating out of my hand again, but I pulled my hand away from her. She put her front feet on my fingers as I pulled my hand away slowly. I kept this up until I had her walking on the brick with her hind feet.

The fourth day, I had her jumping up on the planter to a cup. I kept moving closer to my bench. I finally got her to come up the ramp to my lap. She would relapse from time to time, and I would have to coax her back to the ramp. We became good friends. This is why I called her "Dumb Shit." She was the hardest to train of all my chipmunks. Her sibling would not follow the seed trail at all. I named her sibling without training, a first for me. Guess what I called him. Yep! "Dumb Shit-2." He disappeared in a few weeks. I had no chance to find out if it was a he or she.

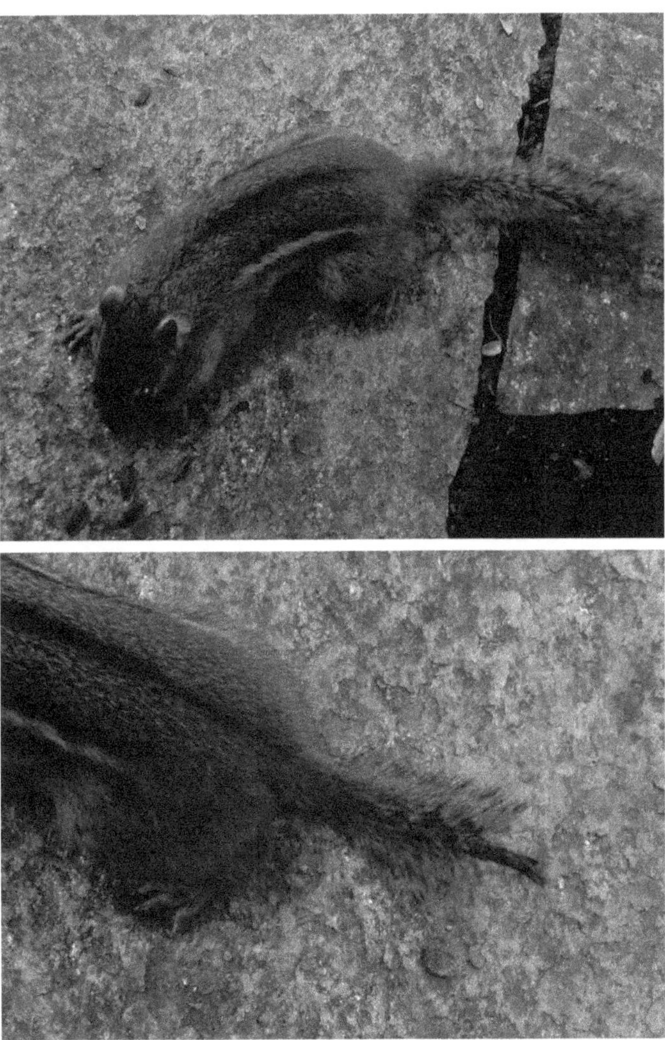

Lost her tail

CARETAKER

LIVED TWO YEARS

The chipmunks in this chapter are "Caretaker," male, lived two years; "Duke," male, eight years old, still living; "Cautious," female, lived two years; and "Princess," female, lived six years.

"Caretaker" did not fit the normal description of a chipmunk.

"Caretaker" took care of "Duke" when "Duke" was very sick. "Caretaker" lived in the same burrow as "Duke" even after "Duke" recovered. They used the same entrance, which was under the back doorstep on the left side. It was about a month after "Duke's" recovery when "Caretaker" dug a new entrance on the right side of the step, which is eight feet long by two feet deep. Over the rest of the summer "Caretaker" enlarged his domain. He piled dirt outside of his new entrance. When the pile got deep, I would remove the dirt. I used a five-gallon bucket to measure the volume of dirt removed. When "Caretaker" finished, I had removed a total of fifteen gallons of dirt. That is a lot of dirt for a chipmunk to move by its cheek pouches. To put this in perspective, think of putting fifteen one-gallon cartons of milk on your table.

In the meantime, "Duke" closed the left-side entrance with dirt and dug a new entrance for himself behind the air conditioner on the west side of the patio. I removed ten gallons of dirt for "Duke" that summer.

"Caretaker" and I bonded late spring when "Duke" was still missing, and I thought "Duke" was dead. "Caretaker" found a feeding position he liked. He positioned himself on my right leg next to my body, looking out over the yard. I would put my right hand over him and feed him with my left hand. The weather can be chilly this time of the year, so I would wear a sweater. When "Caretaker" got in his position, instead of my hand, I put the end of my sweater over him, only his head stuck out. As the weather got warmer, he started jumping into "Cautious's" north feeding station. Well, "Cautious" and I would not stand for this, so I trained "Caretaker" the word NO. "Caretaker" did not like this word but finally submitted. I then trained "Caretaker" to the center feeding station, which belonged to "Princess," who was killed by a hawk. "Cautious" learned that she could eat out of her bowl while "Caretaker" was eating out of his bowl without being attacked.

The next spring started out as usual, but later in the spring, "Caretaker" started greeting me on the woodpile and watched me set up the feeding stations. I thought of how nice it was to be greeted. He waited until I sat down to come to his station. Everything seemed fine except I had fewer and fewer chipmunks come to eat. One morning, I watched out of a window before going outside and saw "Caretaker" savagely attacking a chipmunk. He chased her all the way out of the yard. I saw a pattern. "Caretaker" would hide in the woodpile, under the flowers, under bushes, and attack other chipmunks. He ambushed "Duke" one morning. I hollered NO at "Caretaker," and he did stop the chase, but after that, he attacked over and over but never in the park area. I started getting up from my bench and hollering "NO, GO HOME" and pointing at him. This worked for a while, then he quit and went home. I stepped up the game. I not only got up, but I chased him all the way home. I stepped up the pressure again. When "Caretaker" got in one of his hiding positions, I attacked him, telling him to go home. I was chasing him home and stomping on his entrance. "Caretaker" turned into a true terrorist. A chipmunk gone bad—I did not know that things like this could happen in the chipmunk world. He was so normal in his first year. "Caretaker" moved on. The burrow remained empty for about a month, then "Digger" moved in. "Digger" has an interesting chapter in this book.

It took about four days before all the chipmunks came back.

R.I.P.

DIGGER

LIVED TWO YEARS

Digger's summer burrow

"Digger" was a daughter of "Caretaker." She moved into "Caretaker's" burrow and moved the entrance two feet into the grass. After she was trained, "Digger" would not pick a feeding station. She had no social standing being only months old. If all the stations were occupied, she would attack any chipmunk in their feeding station. She was a chip off the old block. "Digger" would lie in wait for a chipmunk to be going to the park, then attack. I started training her the word NO, but she resisted. I resorted to restricting "Digger" to "Princess's" bowl, as "Princess" was dead. I found that I had to resort to flicking my finger into her side to get her attention instead of a two-finger push. This worked, she bared her teeth at me twice. I flicked her each time, said NO, and pointed at her. Believe it or not, this worked, but only in the park area. She knew the word NO. I ended up chasing her home many times, just like her father, "Caretaker." "Digger" finally left. It took about a week for the rest of the chipmunks to come back.

I guess this counts as the second terrorist in many years. Could this be the COVID-19 influence? Just kidding!

This is a chipmunk I will not miss!

POCKETS

LIVED TWO YEARS

"Pockets" was a male chipmunk with a mission: black seed. He came for seed on my left, across the top of the storage bin. "Duke" owned the top of the storage bin, and you just do not mess with "Duke" the godfather. "Pockets" had it made when "Duke" was not there, but when "Duke" was there, he chased all chipmunks off the top of the bin.

When "Pockets" got chased off the top of the bin, he would come around the ramp and jump in my hand with the cup. I do not know why "Pockets" kept trying to come across the bin top when he knew "Duke" would attack.

Finally I got the idea to use my left arm as a divider between the two. When "Pockets" jumped down from the woodpile, I would put my arm down behind "Duke" so he would not attack "Pockets." After a few times, "Duke" understood that I was feeding "Pockets" his own food. I kept moving the cup closer to me. Soon, I had "Pockets" eating out of the cup on the woodpile behind me. Then I moved him to my shoulder. I put a second cup in my left shirt pocket and tried to get him to transfer to the pocket cup. This took a lot of patience. One day, on his own, he jumped to my shoulder from the woodpile. "Pockets" looked at me eye to eye, I guess to make sure this move was okay. He then stretched down to my pocket with the seed cup. From then on, he was on his own. I would be feeding other chipmunks and would feel "Pockets" pounce on my shoulder and go to my pocket. I would make sure that I pet him. There were many times I would use my cheek to comb his fur with my beard stubble. I had two years with "Pockets." After that I had a whole season with no chipmunk in my pocket. Then along came "Ring Tail." See the chapter on "Ring Tail."

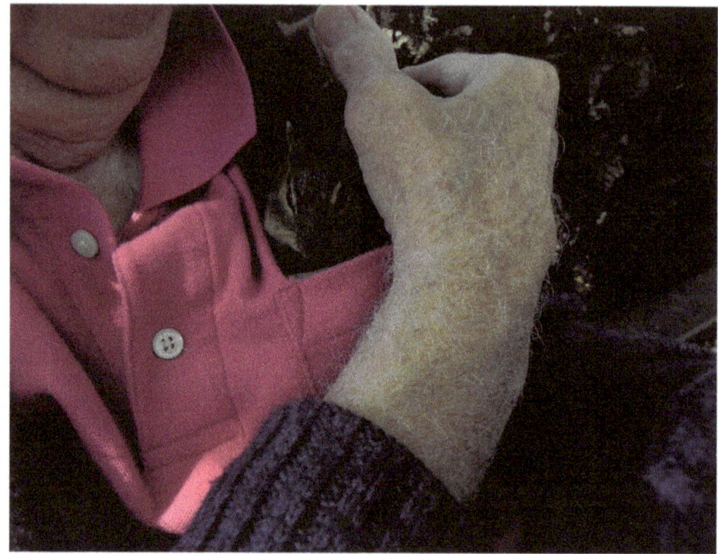

Petting Pockets at her feeding station

RING TAIL

LIVED TWO YEARS

"Ring Tail" and "Split Tail" were siblings. I never knew their mother. They came from the waterfall area. When the siblings were kicked out, "Ring Tail" moved to a new burrow in the east house under a window well near their barbecue grill. "Split Tail" set up home behind the waterfall. "Split Tail" quit coming in early fall. I suspect that the yard of death got her.

"Ring Tail" was the average chipmunk, she came up the ramp to the cup in my lap on a regular basis. If the cups were occupied, she would scrounge around the park area until a cup was free, then up she would come. I would pick her up with the cup and talk to her nose to nose. She was very trusting. I decided that she would be a great candidate for the pocket.

I got her to transfer from the cup to the pocket with very little trouble; however, I had to bring "Ring Tail" and her cup up to my pocket before she would switch. It took her over a week to come to my pocket by herself.

One morning, on her own, she came across the storage bin while "Duke" was not there and jumped up to my shoulder then down to my pocket. YAH! She did this all on her own.

When "Duke" was at his station on top of the storage bin, "Ring Tail" learned to use the woodpile to jump to my shoulder then down to my pocket.

I now had another chipmunk trained to my pocket. Just like I did "Pockets," I petted "Ring Tail" and groomed her with my cheek.

"Ring Tail" had other obstacles to overcome. The neighbors to the east got a second dog, a puppy. When the puppy was let out, "Ring Tail" could not cross the yard to come to eat without being chased. "Ring Tail" figured out a new route to me. She went south along the foundation of the east house to a fence, which runs east–west. She turns west and runs to another fence that goes north–south. She takes the fence north, behind the waterfall, to the highway and takes the highway north to the woodpile. You know the rest; she ends up in my pocket. A long way around for safety. This was her life.

The next season started in March as usual. I open the feeding stations in the morning and never know who will come out of hibernation or when. The chipmunks could arrive between the first and fifteenth of March.

I had been feeding chipmunks for days when "Ring Tail" came out of hibernation. Without any warning, WHAM! She was on my shoulder, looking in my pocket, which was empty. She gave me her disapproval look, and I quickly got a cup with seed up to her. After that I got the pocket prepared for her.

"Ring Tail" and I had a great spring and summer, then she quit coming. My belief is that the new puppy got "Ring Tail." She is another chipmunk I will always remember.

Whispering to Ring Tail

ACROBAT

LIVED THREE MONTHS

"Acrobat" was easy to train. Once she was trained to the cup, she never went through ramp training. In fact, her training was done as far as she was concerned. The target was the cup and only the cup. She focused on either cup as long as it was unoccupied in any position. She never went to a bowl or pocket. Cup-cup-cup that was it.

2 at once—Acrobat is in my lap, Bill is on ramp

She came without warning, no prancing around. She did not care who I was feeding or which hand the cup was in as long as there was no chipmunk already there. If a cup was unoccupied, she would jump to that cup over other chipmunks, even off their backs. "Acrobat" was so fast, the other chipmunks did not have time to react. She would be gone. "Acrobat" never picked a fight.

I could have my left elbow resting on the arm of my bench, straight up in the air, holding a cup and "Acrobat" would jump to my arm and scramble up to the cup. I could play with her by extending my arm straight up in the air over my head and swing my arm left and right. She would hang on and eat. I could gently shake the cup and she would continue eating. She was a true acrobat. "Acrobat" only lasted for about three months. I miss her fearless antics. "Acrobat" was fun to play with.

NEWBE-3

LIVED TWO YEARS

"Newbe-3" was one of a set of three. My only triplets so far. I named them "Newbe-1," "Newbe-2," and "Newbe-3." I did not know the mother, but the father was probably "Duke." He serviced the waterfall area.

The triplets played in and around the bushes near the park. It was fun watching them pounce on each other. Sometimes all three would roll around in a ball. I never saw their mother.

As they grew older, they figured out who is the leader and who is the runt. "Newbe-1" was the dominant one; "Newbe-2" was the follower; and "Newbe-3" was the runt. Everyone chased "Newbe-3."

I trained all three. As the season moved on, they all went their separate ways. "Newbe-1" went to the east house lot, "Newbe-2" went to the waterfall area, and "Newbe-3" went to the south house lot. Later, "Newbe-3" moved to the south side of the patio. She dug a new entrance to "Duke's" old burrow, which he recently abandoned to take over "King's" burrow. The chipmunk shuffled. That fall, I trained them to eat on the patio glider. "Duke" ate out of his cup on my left, and "Newbe-3" ate out of her cup on my right.

OBSERVATION: In all probability, "Duke" is the father of "Newbe-3," giving her the right to "Duke's" burrow.

You may ask, how come "Newbe-1" or "Newbe-2" did not take over "Duke's" burrow? Both were superior to "Newbe-3." Simple answer, both died. That is the chipmunk shuffle.

"Newbe-3" did a strange thing. When she came for seed, she would shell the seed first, then store the meat in her cheeks. That was a first for me. The seed would store much better in the shell. "Newbe-3" could hold a whole cup of seed like that in her cheeks. I was covered in shell fragments when she left. I did not think she would survive the winter because I thought the shelled seeds would rot.

Come spring, she came back. Later that spring, I was feeding "Newbe-3" on the patio glider when I noticed that she was uncomfortable, slow, and very pregnant. When she jumped into my hand, she no longer settled in the palm of my hand. She spread her hind feet out and straddled my right hand that was holding the cup. Her left hind foot was on my ring finger, and her right hind foot was in the palm of my hand. Both of her front feet were on the rim of the cup. This is how she ate. It took her about ten minutes per round trip. After four or five round trips, I dozed off with the cup in my right hand, in my lap, and my left hand over the cup. I woke up when "Newbe-3" jumped on my right leg. When I opened my eyes, there she was staring at me. We made eye contact. She poked my left hand with her nose and looked at me again. I talked to her and removed my left hand so she could eat. "Newbe-3" came back two more times.

"Newbe-3" never showed me her babies; however, she had her second set of babies around August and brought them out many times for me to see while she trained them. As it turned out, one of them was "Squeak."

"Newbe-3" went into hibernation that year and never came back.

Newbe-3 at her feeding station

SQUEAK

TWO YEARS OLD, STILL LIVING

One morning, early spring, I was feeding the chipmunks. A chipmunk came up behind me on the woodpile and squeaked. I turned to find a new chipmunk looking at me; she squeaked again. I clicked at her softly and offered her a cup of seed. She squeaked, jumped down, and came to the cup just as if I had trained her. I watched her go home. She went to the south side of the patio, "Newbe-3's" old burrow.

"Newbe-3" did not make in through the winter. The year before she showed me her two fall babies many times. As I have observed many times, the strongest sibling will take over the mother's burrow upon her death, so "Squeak" took over her mother's burrow and moved the entrance.

Baby Squeak and her sibling

"Squeak" kept coming back, up the ramp, to my right leg, and into the right-hand cup. If the feeding cup was occupied, "Squeak" would jump to the south bowl feeding station, which was "Newbe-3's" dedicated feeding station. Out of seven feeding stations, "Squeak" just happened to choose her mother's station. I can't believe that all this was chance.

Something else very interesting happened. "Squeak" would nibble my finger on her first trip in the morning, just like her mother. Not bite, but nibble on the first trip to me in the morning.

Now for those of you that think "Squeak" is "Newbe-3," you would be very wrong! "Newbe-3" was almost three years old, female, and had many babies. I hold all trained chipmunks in the palm of my hand and wrap my fingers around their bodies. From this, I can tell their age (see the chapter on physical description). "Squeak" is less than one year old, very small, and still growing.

OBSERVATION: When "Squeak" first came up behind me with her baby squeak, I believe she was cautiously asking if I was the right person for seed. Once established, she greeted me every morning with a good morning salutation, the nibble.

CONCLUSION

I know I have learned a lot from these little critters. I have tried to convey this information to you. I hope this book inspired you enough to go out and train your own chipmunks. You now have some insight to the chipmunk society. This should give you an easier start in training. You don't have to take training to the depth I did. My training was to get to know the society and what makes it tick.

You can train your chipmunks just for pleasure. I do recommend that you give your chipmunks a name, this makes it more personal.

You have a jump start on training. You have learned the following:

1. Supply them with black sunflower seed.
2. Use a cup for feeding.
3. Provide dedicated feeding stations and positions.
4. Make and keep eye contact.
5. Whisper to them.
6. Give each chipmunk petting time.
7. Treat them as an individual.

Remember the young ones are teenagers until they survive their first hibernation. They get smarter with age.

GOOD LUCK!

ABOUT THE AUTHOR

Victor was born in Virginia and raised in Southern California. He studied high school in Alabama and college at Auburn University in Alabama. He worked for the Army Rocket and Guided Missile Agency (ARGMA) at Huntsville, Alabama. He later became a regional manager for Spectradyne Inc. in Chicago, Illinois.

With Victor's extensive background in electronics, electrical, mechanical, pneumatics, thermodynamics, and vector analysis, he was hired by Tapecoat Inc. as the process control systems designer, builder, and programmer. He has a patent for the multi-million dollar machine built on site. Victor retired at age seventy-five.

Victor has traveled to thirty-three states including Hawaii and lived in five states. His hobbies are woodworking, welding, stained glass, landscaping, gardening, and training chipmunks. He has been retired for seven years and studied chipmunks for twelve years.

* 9 7 9 8 8 8 6 4 4 2 4 3 4 *